A Tale of
Three Kings

A Tale of
Three Kings
by Gene Edwards

 **CHRISTIAN BOOKS**
AUGUSTA, MAINE

Dedication

To the brokenhearted Christians coming out of authoritarian groups whom we find at our doorstep seeking solace, healing and hope. May you somehow recover and go on with Him who is liberty.

And to Christians who have been, or presently are, involved in the heart-rending experience of a division within your fellowship. May this story give you light or clarity or comfort. And may you, too, somehow recover and go on with Him who is peace.

And may both be so utterly healed that you can still answer the call of Him who asks for all because He is all.

Acknowledgement

To Helen, Carman and Patty for aiding in the preparation of this manuscript; and to Brad, who did the typesetting.

Author's Preface

Why this book and what is its purpose? The answer can probably be traced to my postman. I carry on correspondence with Christians from all parts of North America and, to a lesser degree, from Europe. Recently, a growing number of Christians have been writing, calling (or coming to visit) who have a problem that is of only recent historical origin. I speak of believers who have been devastated by the authoritarian movement that has become so popular with many evangelical groups during the last decade. Now, within the last two or three years, a reaction to this totalitarian concept has set in. A mass exodus is presently under way. The stories being told by these spiritual fugitives are often terrifying and sometimes unbelievable. I am not at all sure it is the doctrine itself that is causing such wide-spread carnage so much as it is the practice of this doctrine. Whatever it is, in over thirty years as an evangelical Christian minister, I have never seen anything that has damaged so many believers so deeply.

My concern is for this multitude of confused, brokenhearted and often bitter Christians who now find their spiritual lives in shambles and who are groping about for even the slightest word of hope.

This emphasis on submission and authority in evangelical circles is still too recent a thing to have produced *any* literature to balance or temper it, and certainly there is nothing in print to comfort or counsel these virtually destroyed Christians. This book, I trust, will serve in some small way to meet this need.

(The only work I know in the English language to recommend is Orwell's little classic, *Animal Farm*. I urge—even implore—every leader who is in a group that emphasizes submission and authority to read this book*. I also recommend it for those who have left or have been excommunicated from such groups.)

There is one thing, dear reader, this book is most certainly not intended to be. It is not intended to be additional fodder in your cannon to better blast your adversaries. I would beg you to be done with such ancient and brutish ways. No, this book is intended for personal and private retreat.

This final word: *A Tale of Three Kings* has a companion volume entitled *Letters to a Devastated Christian*, and was specifically penned to give practical advice to Christians who have been shipwrecked on the rocks of authoritarianism and division.

---

*Publisher's note: This book is often not easy to locate; for this reason Christian Books keeps a supply of them in stock. Write us for details.

I trust both volumes will sound a note, even if heard ever so distantly, of hope.

Gene Edwards
Quebec City, Canada

A Tale of Three Kings

They have set up kings, but not by me: they have made princes, and I knew it not . . . . Hosea 8:4

Well, dear reader, we meet again. How nice to be with you once more. It is a privilege to spend this time with you. We had better go in immediately—they have already dimmed the house lights.

There are two seats, and they're not too far from the stage. Quickly, let us take them.

I understand the story is a drama. I trust, though, you will not find it sad.

I believe we will find the story to be in two parts. In Part One we shall meet an older king, Saul by name, and a young shepherd boy called David. In Part Two we shall once more meet an older king and a young man. But this time the older king is David and the young man is Absalom.

The story is a portrait (you might prefer to call it a rough charcoal sketch) of submission and authority within the Kingdom of God.

They have turned off the lights. That means the actors have taken their places. The audience has quieted itself. There. The curtain is rising.

Our story has begun.

Prologue

The almighty, living God turned to Gabriel. "Go, take these two portions of My being. There are two destinies waiting. To each of them give one portion of Myself."

Carrying two shimmering, glowing, pulsating lights of Life, Gabriel opened the door into the realm between two universes and disappeared. He had stepped into The Mall of Unborn Destinies.

The Archangel addressed those waiting to *be.*

"I have here two portions of the nature of God. The first is the very cloth of His nature. When wrapped about you, it clothes you with the breath of God. As water surrounds one who is within the sea, so does His very breath envelop you. With this, *the wind that clothes,* you will have his power—power to subdue armies, shame the enemies of God and accomplish His work on the earth. Here is the power of God as a gift. Here is immersion into the Spirit."

A destiny stepped forward: "This portion of God is for me."

"True," replied the angel. "And remember, whoever receives such a portion as this will be known by many. Ere your earthly pilgrimage is done, your true character will be known. Such is the destiny of all who wear and wield this portion, for it touches only the outward man, affecting the inner man not one whit.''

The first destined one received and stepped back.

Gabriel spoke again.

''I have here the second of two elements of the Living God. This is not a gift but an inheritance. A gift is worn on the outer man. An inheritance is planted deep inside—like a seed. Yet, even though it is such a small planting, this planting grows and, in time, fills all the inner man.''

Another destiny stepped forward. ''I believe this element is to be mine for my earthly pilgrimage.''

''True,'' responded the angel again. ''I must tell you that what has been given you is a glorious thing—the only element in the universe known to God or angels that can change the human heart. Yet, even this very element of God cannot accomplish its task nor can it grow and fill your entire inner being unless it be compounded well. It must be mixed lavishly with pain, sorrow and crushing.''

The second destined one received and stepped back.

Beside Gabriel sat the recording angel. He dutifully entered into his ledger the record of the two destinies. "And who shall these destinies become after they go through the door to the visible universe?" asked the recording angel.

Gabriel replied softly, "Each in his time shall be a king."

Part One

Chapter I

The youngest son of any family bears two distinctions: He is considered to be both spoiled and uninformed. Usually, little is expected of him. Inevitably, he displays fewer characteristics of leadership than the other children in the family. He never leads; he only follows, for he has no one younger than he on whom to practice leadership.

As it is today, so it was three thousand years ago in a village called Bethlehem, in a family of eight boys. The first seven sons of Jesse worked near their father's farm. The youngest was sent on treks into the mountains to graze the family's small flock of sheep.

On those pastoral jaunts, this youngest son always carried two things: a sling and a small, guitar-like musical instrument. Spare time for a sheepherder is abundant on rich mountain plateaus where sheep graze for days in one sequestered meadow. But as time passed and days became weeks, the young man became very lonely. The feeling of friendlessness that always roamed around inside him was magnified. He often cried. He played his harp a lot. He had a good voice, so he also sang a lot. When these failed to solace him, he gathered up a pile of stones and, one by one, swung them at a distant tree with something akin to fury. When one rockpile was dissipated, he would walk to the blistered tree, reassemble his rocks and designate yet another leafy enemy at yet a farther distance. He engaged in many such solitary battles.

This slingsman-singer-shepherd also loved his Lord. At night, when all the sheep lay sleeping, and he sat staring at the dying fire, he would strum upon his harp and break into a concert of one. He sang the ancient hymns of his forefathers' faith. While he sang, he wept, and while weeping he often broke forth in abandoned praise until mountains in distant places picked up his praise and tears and passed them on to higher mountains still, from whence they eventually were cast up to the ears of God.

When he did not praise and when he did not cry, he tended to each and every lamb and sheep. When not occupied with them, he swung his companionable sling and swung it again and again until he could tell every rock precisely where it was to go.

Once, while singing his lungs out to God, angels, sheep and passing clouds, he spied a living enemy: a huge bear! David lunged forward. Both found themselves moving furiously toward the same small object, a lamb feeding at a table of rich, green grass. Youth and bear stopped half way and whirled to face one another. Even as he automatically searched his pocket for a stone, the young man realized, "Why, I am not afraid." Then he married rock to leather. Meanwhile, brown lightning on mighty, furry legs charged at him

2

with foaming madness. Impelled by the
strength of youth, a brook-smooth pebble
whined through the air to meet that charge.

A few moments later, the man, not quite so
young as a moment before, picked up the little
ewe and said, "I'm your shepherd and God
mine."

And so, long into the night, he wove the day's
saga into a song. He hurled that song to the
skies again and again until he had taught the
melody and words to every angel that had
ears. They, in turn, became custodians of the
song and passed it on as healing balm to
brokenhearted men in every age to come.

Chapter II

A figure in the distance was running toward him. It grew and became his brother.

"Run!" cried the brother. "Run with all your strength. I'll watch the flock."

"Why?"

"An old man, a sage. He wants to meet all eight of the sons of Jesse and he has seen all but you."

"But why?"

"Run!"

David ran. He stopped long enough to get his breath. Then, sweat pouring down his sunburned cheeks, his red face matching his red curly hair, he walked into his father's house, his eyes recording everything in sight.

The youngest son of Jesse stood there, tall and strong, but more in the eyes of the curious old gentleman than anyone else in the room. Kin cannot always tell when a man is grown, even when looking straight at him. The elderly man saw. And something else, too. Some way the old man knew what God knew.

God had taken a house-to-house survey of the whole kingdom in search of something very special. As a result of this survey the Lord God Almighty had found that this leather-lunged singer loved Him with a purer heart than anyone else on all the sacred soil of Israel.

"Kneel," said the bearded one with his waist-long, gray hair. Almost regally, for one who had never been in that particular position before, he knelt, and felt oil pouring down his head and onto his face. Somewhere in one of the closets of his mind labelled "childhood information," a thought was recalled: "This is what men do to make royalty! Samuel is making me a . . . what?"

The Hebrew words were unmistakable. Even children knew them.

"Behold the Lord's anointed!"

Quite a day in the life of that young man, wouldn't you say? Then do you find it strange that this most remarkable event led the young man, not to the throne, but to a decade of hellish agony and suffering? On that day, David was enrolled, not into the lineage of royalty, but into the school of submission.

Samuel went home. The sons of Jesse, save one, went forth to war. The youngest, not yet ripe for war, did, nonetheless, receive a promotion in his father's home . . . from sheepherder to busboy. His new job now was to run food to his brothers on the front lines. He did this regularly.

6

On one such visit to the warfront, he killed
another bear, in the exact same way as he had
the first. This bear, however, was nine feet tall
and human. As the result of this unusual feat,
young David found himself a folk hero.

And eventually he found himself in the castle
of a mad king.

Chapter III

David sang to the mad king. Often. It helped
the old man greatly. And all over the castle,
when David sang, everyone stopped in the
corridors of the king's palace, turned their
ears in the direction of the king's chamber,
and listened and wondered. How did such a
young man come in possession of such won-
derful words and music? Everyone's favorite
seemed to be the song the little lamb had
taught him. They loved that song every bit as
much as the angels did.

Nonetheless, the king was not sane and, therefore, he was jealous. Or was it the other way
around? Either way, the king felt threatened
by David, as kings and others often do when
there is a popular, promising young man
beneath them. The king also knew, as did
David, that this boy just might have his job
some day. But whether David would ascend to
the throne by fair means or foul, Saul did not
know. This question is one of the things that
drove the king mad.

David was caught in a very uncomfortable
position; however, within his circumstance he
seemed to grasp a deep understanding of the
unfolding drama he had been caught up in. He
seemed to understand something that few of
even the wisest men of his day understood.
Something which even in our day, when men
are wiser still, fewer understand.

God did not have, but wanted very much to have, men who would live in pain.

God wanted a broken vessel.

Chapter IV

The mad king saw David as a threat to *his* kingdom. He did not know that God should be left to decide what kingdoms survive which threats. Not knowing this, Saul did what all mad kings do. He threw spears at David. He could. *He* was king. Kings can do things like that. They almost always do. Kings claim the right to throw spears. Everyone knows such men have that right. Everyone knows very, very well. How do they know? Because the king has told them so—many, many times.

What about your king? Is he the Lord's anointed? Maybe he is. Maybe he isn't. No one can ever really know for sure. Men say they are sure. Even *certain*. But they are not. They do *not* know. God knows. But He won't tell.

If your king is truly the Lord's anointed, and if he *also* throws spears, then there are some things you *can* know, and know for sure:

Your king is quite mad.

And he is a king after the order of King Saul.

Chapter V

God has a university. It's a small school. Few enroll, even fewer graduate. Very, very few indeed.

God has this school because He does not have broken men.

Instead He has several other types of men. He has men who claim to be God's authority . . . and aren't; men who claim to be broken . . . and aren't. And men who *are* God's authority, but who are mad. And He has, regretfully, a spectroscopic mixture of everything in between. All of these He has in abundance; but broken men, hardly at all.

In God's sacred school of submission and brokenness, why are there so few students? Because all who are in this school must suffer much pain. And as you might guess, it is often the unbroken ruler (whom God sovereignly picks) who metes out the pain. David was once a student in this school, and Saul was God's chosen way to crush David.

As the king grew in madness, David grew in understanding. He knew that God had placed him in the king's palace, under true authority.

The authority of King Saul, *true?* Yes, God's chosen authority. *Chosen for David.* Unbroken authority, yes. But divine in ordination, nonetheless.

Yes, *that* is possible.

David drew in his breath, submitted to his mad king, and moved farther down the path of his earthly hell.

Chapter VI

David had a question: What do you do when someone throws a spear at you?

Doesn't it seem strange that David would not know the answer? After all, everyone else in the world knows what to do when a spear is thrown at them. Why, you throw it right back!

History answers David's question for him.

"When someone throws a spear at you, David, just wrench it right out of the wall and throw it back. Absolutely everyone else does, you can be sure."

And in doing this small feat you will prove many things: You are courageous. You stand for the right. You boldly stand against the wrong. You are tough and can't be pushed around. You will not stand for injustice or unfair treatment. You are the defender of the faith, keeper of the flame, detector of all heresy. You will not be wronged. All of these attributes then combine to prove that you are obviously a candidate for kingship. Yes, perhaps *you* are the Lord's anointed.

After the order of King Saul.

There is also a possibility that some 20 years after your coronation, *you* will be the most incredibly skilled spear thrower in all the realm. And, most assuredly, by then . . .

Quite mad.

Chapter VII

Unlike anyone else in spear-throwing history, David did *not* know what to do when a spear was thrown at him. He did not throw Saul's spears back at him. Nor did he make any spears of his own and throw them. Something was different about David. All he did was dodge.

What can a man, especially a young man, do when the king decides to use him for target practice? What if he decides not to return the compliment? First of all, he must pretend he can't see spears. Even when they are coming straight at him. Secondly, he must also learn to duck very quickly. Lastly, he must pretend nothing at all happened.

You can easily tell when someone has been hit by a spear. He turns a deep shade of bitter.

David never got hit. Gradually, he learned a very well kept secret. He discovered three things that prevented him from ever being hit. One, never learn anything about the fashionable, easily-mastered art of spear throwing. Two, stay out of the company of all spear throwers. And three, keep your mouth tightly closed.

In this way, spears will never touch you, even when they pierce your heart.

Chapter VIII

"My king is mad. At least, I perceive him so. What can I do?"

Do as David did. Stay, as David did, in the king's court as long as you can. After all, you cannot tell (none of us can) who is the Lord's anointed and who is not. And some kings, whom all will swear are after the order of King Saul, are really after the order of David. And others, whom all men swear are after the order of David, really belong to the order of King Saul. Who is correct? Who can know? To whose voice do you listen? No man is wise enough ever to break that riddle. All any of us can do is walk around asking ourselves the question:

"Is this man the Lord's anointed, and if so, is he after the order of Saul?"

Memorize that question very well. You may have to ask it of yourself 10,000 times. Especially if you are a citizen of a realm whose king just might be mad.

Asking this question may not seem difficult. But it is. Especially when you are crying very hard . . . and dodging spears. And being tempted to throw one back . . . and being encouraged by others to do just that. And all your rationality and sanity and logic and intelligence and common sense agree. But remember in your tears: You know only the question, not the answer.

No one knows the answer.

Except God.

And He *never* tells.

Chapter IX

"I did not like that last chapter. It skirted the problem. I'm in David's situation, and I am in agony. What do I do when the kingdom I'm in is ruled by a spear-wielding king? What does a man *do* in the middle of a knife-throwing contest?"

Well, if you didn't like the question found in the last chapter, you won't like the answer found in this one.

The answer is, "You get stabbed to death."

"What is the necessity of that? Or the good of it?"

You have your eyes on the wrong King Saul. As long as you look at your king, you will blame him and him alone for your present hell. Be careful, for God has *His* eyes fastened sharply on another King Saul. Not the visible one standing up there throwing spears. No, God is looking at *another* King Saul. One just as bad—or worse.

God is looking at the King Saul in *you.*

"In me?!"

Saul is in your bloodstream, in the marrow of your bones. He makes up the very flesh and muscle of your heart. He is mixed into your soul. He inhabits the nuclei of your atoms.

King Saul is one with you.

You are King Saul!

He breathes in the lungs and beats in the breast of us all. There is only one way to get rid of him. He must be annihilated.

You may not particularly find this to be a compliment, but at least now you know why God put you under someone who just *might* be King Saul.

David the sheepherder would have grown up to become King Saul II, except that God cut away the Saul inside David's heart. The operation, by the way, took years and was a brutalizing experience that almost killed the patient. And what were the scalpel and tongs God used to remove this inner Saul?

God used the outer Saul.

King Saul sought to destroy David, but his only success was that he became the hand-maiden of God to put to death the Saul who roamed about in the caverns of David's own heart. Yes, it is true that David was virtually destroyed in the process, but this had to be. Otherwise the Saul in him would have survived.

David accepted his fate. He embraced the cruel circumstances. He lifted no hand, nor offered resistance. Nor did he grandstand his piety. Silently, privately, he bore the crucibles. Because of this he was deeply wounded. His whole inner being was mutilated. His personality was altered.

When the gore was over, David was barely recognizable.

You weren't satisfied with the question in the last chapter? Then you probably didn't like the answer in this one.

None of us do.

Except God.

Chapter X

How does a man know when it is finally time to leave the Lord's anointed—especially the Lord's anointed after the order of King Saul?

David never made that decision. The Lord's anointed made it for him. The king's own decree settled the matter! "Hunt him down, kill him like a dog." Only then did David leave. No, he fled. Even then, he never spoke a word or lifted a hand against Saul. Please also note that David did not split the kingdom when he made his departure. He did not take part of the population with him. He left *alone*. Alone. All alone. King Saul II never does that. He always takes those who "insist on coming along."

Yes, men do insist on going with you, don't they? They're willing to help you found the kingdom of King Saul II. Men dare not leave alone.

But David left alone. You see, the Lord's true anointed can leave alone.

All alone.

Chapter XI

Caves are not the ideal place for morale building.

There is a certain sameness to them all, no matter how many you have lived in. Dark. Wet. Cold. Stale. It is even worse when you are in them alone . . . and can hear the dogs baying.

But sometimes, when the dogs and hunters were not near, the prey sang. He started low, then lifted up his voice and sang the song the little lamb had taught him. The cavern walls echoed each note just as the mountain once had done. The music rolled down into deep cavern darkness that became an echoing choir singing back to him.

He had less now than he had when he was a shepherd, for now he had no lyre, no sun, not even the company of sheep. The memories of the court had faded. David's greatest ambition now reached no higher than a shepherd's staff.

He sang a great deal.

And matched each note with a tear.

How strange what suffering begets.

There in those caves, drowned in the sorrow of his song, and in the song of his sorrow, David very simply became the greatest hymn writer, the greatest comforter of broken hearts this world shall ever know.

Chapter XII

He ran—through fields, down slimy riverbeds.
Sometimes the dogs came close; sometimes
they even *found* him. But swift feet, rivers,
and watery pits hid him. He got his food from
the fields, dug roots from the roadside, slept in
trees, hid in ditches, crawled through briars
and mud. For days he ran—not daring to stop
or eat. He drank the rain. Half naked, all
filthy, on he walked, stumbled, crawled and
clawed.

Caves were castles now. Pits were home.

In times past, mothers had always told their
children that if they didn't behave they would
end up like the town drunk. No longer. They
had a better, more frightening story. "Be
good, or you'll end up like the great giant
killer."

In Jerusalem, when men taught of being
submissive to kings and honoring the Lord's
anointed, David was the parable. "See, this is
what God does to rebellious men." The young
listeners shuddered at the thought and som-
berly resolved never to have anything to do
with rebellion.

Much later David would reach a foreign land,
and a small, very small, measure of safety.
Here, too, he was feared, hated, lied about

and plotted against. He shook hands with
murder on several occasions.

These were David's darkest hours. You know
them as his pre-king days, but he didn't. He
assumed this was his lot forever.

Suffering was giving birth. Humility was being
born.

Chapter XIII

Others had to flee as the king's madness grew.
First one, then three, then ten, and eventually
hundreds. After long searching, some of these
fugitives made contact with David. They had
not seen him for a long time.

The truth was that when they did see him
again, they simply didn't recognize him. He
had changed: his personality, his disposition,
his total being had been altered. He talked
less. He loved God more. He sang differently.
They had never heard these songs before.
Some were lovely beyond words. Some froze
the blood in their veins.

Those who found him, and who decided to be
his fellow fugitives were a sorry, worthless lot:
Thieves, liars, complainers, fault-finders,
rebellious men with rebellious hearts. They
were blind with hate for the king and, therefore, for all authority figures. They would have
been troublemakers in paradise, if they could
have gotten in.

David did not lead them. He did not share
their attitudes. Yet, unsolicited, they began to
follow him.

He never spoke to them of authority. He never
spoke of submission; but, to a man, they submitted. He laid down no rules. Legalism is not
a word found in the vocabulary of fugitives.

31

Nonetheless, they cleaned up their outward lives. Gradually, their inward lives began to change, too.

They didn't fear submission or authority; they didn't even think about the topic, much less discuss it. Then why did they follow him? They didn't, exactly. It was just that he was . . . well . . . David. That didn't need explanation.

And so, for the first of two times, true kingship had its nativity.

Chapter XIV

"Why, David, why?"

The place was another nameless cave.

The men stirred about restlessly. Gradually, and very uneasily, they began to settle in. All were as confused as Joab, who had finally voiced the question.

Joab wanted some answers. Now.

David should have seemed embarrassed or at least defensive. He was neither. He was looking past Joab like a man viewing another world that only he could see.

Joab walked directly in front of David, looked down on him, and began roaring his frustrations.

"Many times he almost speared you to death in his castle. I've seen that with my own eyes. Finally, you ran away. Now for years you have been nothing but a rabbit for him to chase. Furthermore, the whole world believes the lies he tells about you. He has come, the King himself, hunting every cave, pit and hole on earth to find you and kill you like a dog. But tonight *you* had *him* at the end of his own spear and you did nothing!

"Look at us. We're animals *again.* Less than an hour ago you could have freed us all. Yes, we could all be free, right now! Free! And Israel, too. She would be free. Why, David, why didn't you end these years of misery?"

There was a long silence. Men shifted again, uneasily. They were not used to seeing David rebuked.

"Because," said David very slowly (and with a gentleness that seemed to say, 'I heard what you asked, but not the way you asked it'), "because once, long ago, he was not mad. He was young. He was great. Great in the eyes of God and men. And it was God who made him king—*God*—not men."

Joab blazed back, "But now he *is mad!* And God is no longer with him. And, David, he will yet kill you!"

This time it was David's answer that blazed with fire.

"Better he kill me than that I learn his ways. I shall not practice the ways that cause kings to go mad. I will not throw spears, nor will I allow hatred to grow in my heart."

Joab could not handle such a senseless answer. He stormed out into the dark.

That night men went to bed on cold, wet stone
and muttered about their leader's distorted,
masochistic views of submission to kings.

Angels went to bed that night too, and
dreamed, in the afterglow of that rare, rare
day, that God might yet be able to give His
authority to a trustworthy vessel.

Chapter XV

What kind of man was Saul? Who was this
one who made himself David's enemy?
Anointed of God. Deliverer of Israel. And yet
remembered mostly for his madness.

Forget the bad press. Forget the stinging
reviews. Forget his reputation. Look at the
facts. Saul was one of the greatest figures of
human history. He was a farm boy, a real
country kid. He was tall, good-looking, and
well-liked.

He was baptized into the Spirit of God.

He also came from a good family; that is, in his
lineage were some of the great historical
figures of all mankind: Abraham, Israel,
Moses. These were his ancestors.

Do you remember the background? Abraham
had founded a nation. Moses had set that
nation free from slavery. Joshua gave those
people a toehold in the land which was
promised to them by God. The judges kept the
whole thing from disintegrating into total
chaos. That's when Saul came along. It was
Saul who took these people and welded them
into a united kingdom.

Saul united a people and founded a kingdom.
Few men have ever done that. He created an

army out of thin air. He won battles in the power of God, defeated the enemy again and again, as few men ever have. Remember that, and remember he was baptized in the Spirit.

And he was a prophet. The Spirit came on him in power and authority. He did and said unprecedented things and it was all by the power of the Spirit.

He was everything men today are seeking to be . . . empowered with the Holy Spirit . . . able to do the impossible . . . for God. A leader, chosen by God with power from God.

Saul was given authority that is God's alone. He was God's anointed and God treated him that way.

He was also eaten with jealousy, capable of murder and willing to live in spiritual darkness. Is there a moral in these contradictions? Yes, and it will splinter a lot of your concepts about power, about great men under God's anointing, and about God Himself.

Many men pray for the power of God. More every year. Those prayers sound powerful, sincere, godly and without ulterior motive. Hidden under this prayer and fervor, however, are ambition, a craving for fame, the desire to be known and envied, the desire to be considered a spiritual giant. The man who prays this way may not even know it, but such things are, nonetheless, in his heart . . . in *your* heart.

38

Even as men pray these prayers, they are hollow inside. There is little internal spiritual growth. Prayer for power is the quick and the short way. It sidesteps, circumnavigates and avoids internal growth.

There is a vast difference in the outward clothing of the Spirit's power and the inward filling of the Spirit's life. The difference is this: In one, the hidden man of the heart is changed. In the other, that monster may very well remain unaltered.

Interesting about God. Even shocking. (He hears those requests for power, you know.) Very often He grants those prayers. Sometimes He says yes to some very unworthy vessels. He gives them power. *His* power, even though they are a pile of dead men's bones inside.

Why does God do such a thing? To reveal to all men, eventually, the state of internal nakedness in that man.

So think again when you hear the power merchant. Remember: God sometimes gives power to men for unseen reasons. A man can be living in the grossest of sin and the outward gift will still be working perfectly. The gifts of God, once given, cannot be recalled. Even in the presence of sin.

Furthermore, some men, living just such lives, *are* the Lord's anointed . . . in the Lord's eyes.

Saul was living proof of this fact.

The gifts cannot be revoked.

Terrifying, isn't it?

If you are young and have never seen this happen, sometime in the next 40 years you will see it: Highly gifted and very powerful men . . . reputed to be leaders in the Kingdom of God . . . you will see them do some awfully dark and ugly deeds.

What does this world need? Gifted men, outwardly empowered? Or broken men, inwardly transformed!

Keep in mind that some of the men who have been given the very power of God have raised armies, defeated the enemy, brought forth mighty works of God, preached and prophesied with unparalleled power and eloquence . . .

And thrown spears,

And hated other men,

And plotted to kill,

And prophesied naked,

And even consulted witches.

Chapter XVI

"You still haven't answered my question. The man I sit under: I think he is a King Saul. How can I know with certainty?"

It is not given to us to know. And remember, even Sauls are the Lord's anointed.

You see, there are always men—everywhere, in every age, in every group—who will stand and tell you: "That man is after the order of King Saul." While another, just as sure, will rise to declare, "No, he is the Lord's anointed after the order of David." No man can *really* know which of the two is correct. And if you happen to be in the balcony looking down at the men screaming at one another, you can wonder to which order, if any, *they* belong.

Remember, your leader may be a David.

"That's impossible!"

Is it? Most of us know at least two men who were in the lineage of David who have been damned and crucified by men who were certain they were *not* Davids.

And if you don't know of two such cases, for sure you know of one.

Men who go after the Sauls sometimes crucify the Davids among us.

Who, then, can know who is a David and who is a Saul?

God knows. But He won't tell.

However, the passing of time (and the behavior of your leader while that time passes) reveals a great deal about your leader.

And the passing of time, and the way you react to that leader—be he David or Saul—reveals a great deal about *you.*

Chapter XVII

Two generations after the reign of Saul, a young man enthusiastically enrolled himself into the ranks of Israel's army under a new king, the grandson of David. He soon began hearing tales of David's mighty men of valor. He determined to discover if one of those mighty men might still be alive and, if so, to find him and talk to him, though he calculated such a one would be a hundred years or more in age.

At last he found there was one such person still alive and, having learned his whereabouts, made haste to his dwelling. Anxiously, if not hesitantly, he knocked on the door. Slowly it opened. There stood a giant of a man, gray . . . no, white haired . . . and wrinkled beyond expectation.

"Are you, sir, one of David's mighty men of long ago—one of those we have heard so much about?"

The old man surveyed the young man's face, his features, his uniform, for a long moment. Then in an ancient but firm voice, he replied, never taking his steady gaze off the young man's face.

"If you are asking if I am a former thief and cave dweller and one who followed a sobbing, hysterical fugitive, then yes, I was one of the 'mighty men of David.'"

He straightened his shoulders with those last words; nonetheless, his sentence ended in a chuckle.

"Why, you make the Great King sound like a weakling. Was he not the greatest of all rulers?"

"He was no weakling," said the old man. Then, sizing up the motivation for the eager young man's presence at his door, he replied wisely and softly, "Nor was he a great leader."

"Then what, good sir? For I have come to learn the ways of the Great King and his . . . uh . . . mighty men. What *was* the greatness of David?"

"I see you have the ambitions typical of youth," said the old warrior. "I have the distinct notion you dream of leading men yourself one day." He paused, then continued reflectively. "Yes, I'll tell you of the greatness of my king, but my words may surprise you."

The old man's eyes filled with tears as he thought first of David and then of the foolish new king only recently crowned.

"I will tell you of my king and his greatness.

"My king never threatened me as does yours. Your new king has begun his reign with laws, regulations and fear. The clearest memory I have of my king when we lived in the caves is that his was a life of *submission*. Yes, he showed me submission, not authority. He taught me, not the quick cures of rules and laws, but the art of patience. *That* is what changed my life. Legalism is nothing but a leader's way of avoiding suffering. Rules were invented by elders, so they could get to bed early! Men who harp on authority only prove they have none. And kings who make speeches about submission only betray the presence of this fear in their hearts: They are not certain they can survive a rebellion.

"David taught me losing, not winning. Giving, not taking. He showed me that the leader, not the follower, is inconvenienced. He shielded us from suffering; he did not mete it out.

"He taught me that authority yields to rebellion, especially when that rebellion is nothing more dangerous than immaturity, or perhaps stupidity." The old man was obviously remembering some very tense and perhaps humorous episodes in the caves.

"No," he said, now in a voice with a touch of eloquence, "authority from God is not afraid of challengers, makes no defense, and cares not one whit if it must be dethroned.

"That was the greatness of the Gre . . . of the *true* King."

The old man began to walk away. Both anger and regality were evident in his bearing as he turned. Then he faced the youth once more, thundering one last salvo: "As far as David's having authority: Men who don't have it talk about it all the time. Submit, submit, that's all you hear. David had authority, but I don't think that fact ever ocurred to him! We were 600 no-goods with a leader who cried a lot. That's all we were!"

Those were the last words the young man heard from the old warrior. Slipping back into the street, he wondered if he would ever be happy serving under Rehoboam.

Chapter XVIII

So, having come to the end of our study of Saul and David, you feel you have been greatly assisted? What's that? You are now certain the man you are under is not truly from God . . . or if he is, he is at best only a Saul? My, how certain we mortals can be . . . of things even angels do not know.

May I ask you then, what you plan to do with this newly acquired knowledge? Yes, I am aware that you yourself are neither a Saul nor a David . . . but only a peasant of the realm. You do plan, though, to share your new findings with a few friends? I see. Perhaps then, I should warn you that with this heady new knowledge of yours there is an inherent danger. A strange mutation can take place within your own heart. You see, it is possible . . . but wait!

What is it I see over there! There! In that distant mist behind you. Do you see? Who is that apparition-like figure making his way through the fog? It seems I have surely seen him before.

Look closely. Is it not possible for us to make out what he is doing?

He appears to be bending over some ancient chest. Yes, he has opened it.

Who is he? And what *is* he doing?

He has drawn something out of the chest. A cloak? It is some kind of cape. Why, he is putting it on! The thing fits him perfectly, falling about his shoulders like a mantle.

Now what? He reaches again into that chest. I know I have seen that person somewhere before. What is it he pulls forth this time? A shield? No, a coat of arms. Yes, a coat of arms from some ancient, long forgotten order. He holds it up as one who would make that order his own! Who is that man! The bearing. The stance. The carriage. I've seen it before. I'm sure.

Ah! He moved out of the mist into the light. We will see him clearly now.

That face. Is it not you?!

Yes. It is. Is is *you!* You who can so wisely discern the presence of an unworthy Saul!

Go! Look in yon mirror. That man is *you!* Look, too, at the name upon that coat of arms.

Behold: ABSALOM THE SECOND!!

Part Two

Chapter XIX

"Look. Here comes David!"

Bright smiles, a few giggles, some light laughter.

"See! It's David, no less."

Again, wide grins, a wave, and quiet amusement.

"That isn't David," exclaimed a youth to his guardian as they walked along the side of the street. "Why do they speak that way?"

"True, child, it is not David. It's only Absalom coming from the gate."

"Why do they call him David?" the boy asked, looking back over his shoulder at the handsome man in the chariot with the 50 men running before him.

"Because he reminds us all of David when he was young. And because we are all so glad there is such a fine young man to take David's place someday. And perhaps, too, because Absalom is even better looking than David. He may be the most handsome man alive."

"Will Absalom be king soon? How old is David, anyway? Is he about to die?"

"Of course not, my boy. Let's see . . . how old is David? Probably about the same age as King Saul when his reign came to an end."

"How old is Absalom?"

"About the same age as David when Saul was trying so hard to kill him."

"David is Saul's age. Absalom is the age of David when he first became king," mused the boy. They walked on silently for a while. The boy, obviously deep in thought, spoke again.

"Saul was very hard on David, wasn't he?" asked the boy pensively.

"Yes, very."

"Is King David going to treat Absalom the same way?"

The guardian paused to consider the question, but the child went on: "If David treats Absalom badly, will Absalom behave as well as David did?"

"Child, the future will surely tell us. My, you ask such questions! If, when you are grown, you can give answers as well as you can now ask questions, you will surely be known as the wisest man on earth."

The two turned into the palace gate.

Chapter XX

It warmed your heart to know a man who saw things so clearly. Discerning. Yes, that was the word that best described him—discerning. He could penetrate to the heart of any problem.

Men felt secure just being with him. They even longed to have time with him. Talking with him, they realized that they themselves were wiser than they'd realized. It made them feel good.

As he discussed solution after solution, men began to long for the day when this one would be their leader. He could right so many wrongs. He gave them a sense of hope.

But this imposing, insightful man would never deliberately hasten the day of his own rule. He was far too humble, too respectful of the present leader. Those around him began to feel a little frustrated that they would have to keep waiting for the better days of this man's rule.

The more they sat in his living room and talked, the more they realized there were things amiss in the present kingdom. Problems were coming to light that they'd never been aware of, never dreamed of before. Yes, they really were growing in wisdom and in insight.

As the days passed, more and more of them came to listen. Word spread quietly. ''Here is one who understands and has the answers.'' The frustrated came. They listened and asked questions. They received excellent answers and began to hope.

Heads nodded. Dreams were born. As time passed, there were more such gatherings. Ideas turned into stories, stories of injustice that others might have deemed trivial. But not this listener! He was compassionate. And as those around him talked, the discovered injustices seemed to grow in number and severity. With each new story, men were more shocked at the unfairness that now, it seemed, was rampant.

But the wise young man sat quietly and added not a word to these murmurings. He was too noble, you see. He always closed the evening conversations with an humble word of deference toward those with responsibility . . . .

At first!

But it was too much to expect that any man could sit quietly by forever. This endless parade of injustice was bound to stir even the most respectful man. Even the purest in heart would be smitten with anger. (And this man was certainly the very purest in heart!)

Such a compassionate man could not forever turn his face from these sufferings nor forever remain silent. Such noble character as this had someday to speak out.

Finally his followers, which he vowed he did not have, were almost livid. Their insights into the wrongdoings of the kingdom abounded. They wanted to do something about it all.

At last it seemed he might concede. At the outset it was only a word. Later, a sentence of agreement. Men's hearts leaped. Glee, if not joy, reigned. Nobility was at last arousing itself to action. But no! He cautioned them not to misunderstand. He was grieved, yes. But he could not speak against those in seats of responsibility. No, absolutely not. No matter how great the grievances, no matter how justified. He would *not*.

Yet he grieved more and more. It was obvious that some reports drove him to agony. Finally, his righteous anger broke out in cool, controlled words of strength. "These things ought not to be." He stood, eyes blazing. "If I were in responsibility, this is what I would do . . . ."

And with these words, the rebellion was ignited. Ignited in all but one, that is. In the noblest and purest man in the room, this was not the case.

Rebellion had been in his heart for years.

Chapter XXI

"Sage!"

"Yes."

"Sage, may I have a moment of your time?"

"Why, of course. I have a great deal of time."

"You have just come from a gathering of friends at Absalom's home?"

"Yes, that is correct."

"Would you mind sharing some of the impressions you had while there?"

"You mean a general impression of Absalom and his friends?"

"Yes, that would be good enough."

"Well, I have met many men like Absalom. Many."

"Then what is he like?"

"He is both sincere and ambitious. A contradiction perhaps, but true, nonetheless. He probably means some of what he says. But his ambition will continue long after he discovers his inability to do the things he promises."

57

"I'm sorry, Sage, I do not understand."

"Two things stand out in my mind. At one gathering, when Absalom was answering questions, he was very emphatic that there should be more freedom in the kingdom. Everyone liked that. 'A people should be led only by God, and not by men,' he said. 'Men should do only what they feel led of God to do.' I believe those were his words.

"At another meeting he spoke of the great visions he had for God's kingdom—of the great achievements the people were capable of. On the other hand, he spoke of many changes he would make in the way the kingdom is run. Although he did not seem to notice it, he had stated two irreconcilable plans.

"Yes indeed, he does remind me of many other men I have encountered over the passing years."

"Sage, I think I understand what you've said, but I'm not sure what your point is."

"Absalom dreams. Dreams of what should be, of what *will* be: 'This is what *I* will do.' But to fulfill those dreams, he must have the peoples' cooperation. Ah, this is the point men overlook. Their dreams rest totally on the premise that the people of God will be with them, that all will see as they see. They can envision no problems in their future kingdom. Possibly the

people *will* be such dreamers; yes, possibly
the people will follow, and possibly they
will not.

"At most, the Lord's people will follow a
leader for a few days. They are never with anyone very long. Generally, people do what they
please. They can be stopped to do someone
else's pleasure for a time, but not for long.
People will not work too hard, even if they are
following *God.*

"There is no kingdom without discord. Even
God had His critics in heaven, you know. All
kingdoms follow a bumpy course. And people,
especially God's people, never follow any
dream in unison. No, to accomplish all he
spoke of tonight will take time. Absalom has
but one recourse: dictatorship. Either that, or
he will see few, if any, of his grand dreams
accomplished. If he does become a dictator,
I can assure you that in the not too distant
future you will be seeing new meetings such
as the one I have just come from tonight . . .
only with new faces, new dreams, and plans
for a new rebellion, this one *against* Absalom!
Then, when *Absalom* hears of such a meeting,
and of discussion about a rebellion, he will
have but one recourse.''

"What do you feel he will do, Sage?"

"Rebels who ascend the throne have little
patience with other rebels and their rebellions.
When Absalom is faced with rebellion, he will

become a tyrant. He will squelch rebellion and rule with an iron hand . . . and by fear. He will eliminate all opposition. This is always the final stage of high-sounding insurrections. Such may be Absalom's lot, if he takes the throne from David.''

''But Sage, have not some rebellions been of benefit, throwing out brutes and despots?''

''Oh, yes, a few. But I remind you: This particular kingdom is different from all others. This kingdom is composed of God's people. It is a spiritual kingdom. I tell you emphatically, no rebellion in the kingdom of God is proper, nor can it ever be fully blessed.''

''Why do you say this, Sage?''

''For many reasons. One is obvious. In the spiritual realm, a man who will lead a rebellion has already proven, no matter how grandiose his words or angelic his ways, that he has a critical nature and an unprincipled character and hidden motives in his heart. Frankly, he is a thief. He creates dissatisfaction and tension within the realm, and then either seizes power or siphons off followers. The followers he gets, he uses to found his own dominion.

''No, God never honors division in His realm.

''I find it curious that men who feel qualified to split God's kingdom do not feel capable of going somewhere else to another land to raise up a completely new kingdom. No, they must steal from another. They seem always to need at least a few pre-packaged followers.

"Beginning bare-handed and empty-handed frightens the best of men.

"There are many lands unspoiled and unpossessed. There are many people in other places waiting to follow a true king, a true man of God. I repeat myself. (There are those who say I often repeat myself.) Why don't 'would-be kings and prophets' simply walk quietly away, alone, find another people in another place, and there raise up the kingdom they envision?

"Men who lead rebellions in the spiritual world are unworthy men. There are no exceptions. And now I must go. I must join the passing parade."

"Tell me, Sage, what is your name?"

"My name? I am History."

Chapter XXII

David stood looking over the wall of the garden terrace of his palace. The lights from the houses in the Holy City twinkled below him. From behind, a man approached. David sighed and without turning, spoke. "Yes, Joab, what is it?"

"Do you know?"

"I know," he replied quietly.

"How long have you known?" asked Joab with anxious surprise.

"For months, years, perhaps a decade. Perhaps I have known for thirty years."

Joab was not sure, after this answer, if they were speaking of the same subject. Absalom, after all, was not much past thirty. "Sir, I speak of Absalom," he said a little hesitantly.

"As do I," said the king.

"If you have known so long, why did you not stop him?"

"I was just asking myself that question, too."

"Shall I stop him for you?"

David whirled round! In one second, Joab's query had resolved his perplexities.

"You shall not! Nor shall you speak one word to him. Nor shall you criticize him. Nor shall you allow anyone else to speak critically of him or of what he is doing."

"But will he not then take the kingdom?"

David sighed again, softly, slowly. For a moment, he balanced between tears and a smile. Then he smiled lightly and said, "Yes, perhaps he will."

"What will you do? Do you have plans?"

"No. None. Quite frankly, I have no idea what to do. I have fought many battles and faced many sieges. I have usually known what to do. But for this occasion, I have only the experience of my youth to draw on. The course I followed at that time seems to me to be the best I can find—at least for the moment."

"And what was it?"

"To do absolutely nothing."

Chapter XXIII

David was alone again. Slowly, quietly, he walked the length of his roof garden. Finally, he paused and spoke aloud to himself.

"I have waited, Absalom; I have waited and watched for years. I have asked again and again, 'What is in the heart of this young man?' And now I know. You will do the unthinkable. You will divide the very kingdom of God. All else was talk."

David was quiet for a moment. Then, almost in awe, he spoke, his voice hushed. "Absalom does not hesitate to divide the *Kingdom of God.*

"Now I know. He seeks followers—at least he does not turn them away. Though he seems magnificently pure and illustriously noble, still he divides. His followers grow, even though he convincingly states that he has none."

For a long time David said nothing. Finally, with a trace of humor in his words, he began to address himself. "All right, good King David, you have one issue resolved. You are in the middle of a division and you may very well be dethroned. Now, to the second issue." He paused, lifted his hand and, almost fatally, asked himself, "What *will* you do?"

"The kingdom hangs in the balance. It seems I have two choices: to lose everything, or to be a Saul to Absalom. In my old age, shall I now become a Saul? I feel the Lord Himself awaits my decision.

"Shall I now be a Saul?" he asked himself again, this time loudly.

A voice from behind him answered, "Good king, he has been no David to you."

David turned. It was Abishai who had approached unannounced.

"A crowded place, this terrace," quipped David.

"Sir?" said Abishai.

"Nothing. Suffice it to say I have not been without visitors today—a day when I would have chosen solitude. What did you say to me? In fact, what did I say?"

"You said, 'Shall I be a Saul to Absalom?' and I replied, 'He has been no young David to you.'"

"I never challenged Saul; I never attempted to divide the kingdom during his reign. Is that what you are saying?"

"More," replied Abishai strongly. "Saul was evil toward you and made your life torture. You responded only with respect and private

agony. The bad things all fell on you. Yet you
could have divided the kingdom and probably
could have overthrown Saul. Rather than do
that, you packed up and left the kingdom. You
fled rather than cause division. You risked
your life for unity and sealed your lips and
eyes to all his injustices. You had more cause
to rebel than any man in the history of this or
any other kingdom that ever has been or ever
shall be. Has Absalom ever behaved like that?
Absalom respecting you? Absalom seeking to
preserve the Kingdom? Absalom refusing to
speak against you? Absalom refusing
followers? Absalom departing the land to
prevent its sundering? Absalom respectful?
Absalom bearing suffering in silent agony?
The bad things falling on Absalom? No, he is
only pure and noble!"

Abishai's last words came out almost in bites.
Then he continued again, more gravely this
time.

"His grievances are minor compared to your
rightful grievances toward Saul. You never
mistreated Saul. And you have never, in any
way, been unfair to Absalom."

David interrupted with a grin. "I seem to have
a gift for making old men and young men hate
me without cause. In my youth, the old attack
me; when I am old, the young attack me. What
a marvelous achievement."

"My point," continued Abishai, "is that
Absalom is no David. Therefore I ask you:

Why don't you stop his rebellion? Stop him, the miserable . . . . ''

"Careful, Abishai. Remember, he is also a son of the king. We should never speak ill of the son of a king."

"Good king, I remind you that you refused to raise your sword or your spear even once against Saul. I repeat myself. Absalom speaks against you night and day. He will one day—soon—raise an army against you. Nay, a nation. *This* nation! Absalom is no David. I counsel you to stop him!''

"You are asking me, Abishai, to become a Saul," David replied heavily.

"No, I'm saying he is no David; stop him!''

"And if I stop him, will I still be a David?'' asked the king, his eyes piercing Abishai. "Abishai, to stop him I must either be a Saul or an Absalom.''

"My king and my friend, I speak to you fondly: I sometimes think you are a bit insane."

"Yes, I can see why," chuckled David.

"Dear king, Saul was a bad king. Absalom is, in some ways, a youthful reincarnation of him. You only are constant. You are forever the brokenhearted shepherd boy. Tell me truthfully, what do you plan?''

"Until now, I have not been sure. Of this I am now certain: In my youth I was no Absalom. In my old age I shall not be a Saul. In my youth, by your own words, I was David. In my old age I intend to be David still. Even if it costs me a throne, a kingdom, and perhaps my head."

Abishai said nothing for a while. Then slowly, he spoke, making sure he grasped the significance of David's decision.

"You were not an Absalom; you will not be a Saul. Sir, if you are not willing to put Absalom down, then I suggest we prepare to evacuate the kingdom, for Absalom will surely rule."

"Only as surely as King Saul killed the shepherd boy," replied the wise old king.

"What?" said Abishai, startled.

"Think on it, Abishai. God once delivered a defenseless shepherd boy from the powerful, mad king. He can yet deliver an old ruler from an ambitious, young rebel."

"You underestimate your adversary," retorted Abishai.

"You underestimate my God," replied David serenely.

"But why, David? Why not fight?"

69

"I will give you the answer. If you will recall—
for you were there—I once gave this same
answer to Joab in a cave long ago! It is better I
be defeated, even killed, than to learn the
ways of . . . of a Saul, *or* the ways of an
Absalom. The kingdom is not *that* valuable.
Let him have it, if that be the Lord's will. I
repeat: I *shall not* learn the ways of Sauls or
Absaloms.

"And now, being an old man, I will add a word
I might not have known then. Abishai, no man
knows his own heart. I certainly do not know
mine. Only God does. Shall I defend my little
realm in the name of God? Shall I throw
spears, and plot and divide . . . and kill men's
spirits if not their bodies . . . to protect my
empire? I did not lift a finger to *stop* a mad
king, nor did I lift a finger to be *made* king.
Now I will still lift none to *remain* king. Nor to
preserve a kingdom. Even the Kingdom of
God! God put me here. It is not my responsibility to take, or keep, authority. I suspect
that, if He chose, God could protect and keep
the kingdom even now. After all, it is *His*
kingdom.

"As I said, no man knows his heart. I do not
know mine. Who knows what is really in my
heart? It may be that in God's eyes I am no
longer worthy to rule. Perhaps He *is* through
with me. Perhaps it is His will for Absalom to
rule. I honestly don't know. But if this is His
will, I wish it. God may be finished with me!

"Any young rebel who raises his hand against one whom he believes to be a Saul; any old king who raises his hand against one whom he believes to be an Absalom, may—in truth—be raising his hand against the will of God.

"Wouldn't I look a little strange trying to stay in control when God was desiring that I fall?"

"But you know that Absalom should not be king!" replied Abishai in frustration.

"Do I? No man knows. Only God knows, and He has not spoken. I will not fight to be king or to remain king. May God come tonight and take the throne, the kingship and . . ." David's voice faltered, " . . . and His *anointing* from me. I seek his will, not His power. I repeat. He may be through with me."

"King David," came a voice from behind the two men.

"Yes? Oh, a messenger. What is it?"

"Absalom. He wishes to see you a moment. He wishes to ask permission to go to Hebron to make a sacrifice."

"David," said Abishai hoarsely, "you know what that really means, don't you?"

"Yes."

"And you know what he will do if you let him go?"

"Yes."

"Will you let him?"

David turned to the messenger. "Tell Absalom I will be there momentarily." David looked one last time at the quiet city below; turned, and walked toward the door.

"*Will* you let him go to Hebron?" Abishai demanded.

"I will," said the king of all kings. "Yes, I will."

Then he turned to the messenger. "This is a dark hour for me. When I have finished speaking to Absalom, I shall retire. Tomorrow have one of the prophets come to me for consultation. Or a scribe. On second thought, send me Zadok, the high priest. Ask him if he would join me here after the evening sacrifice."

Abishai called out once more. Softly this time. Admiration flashed across his face. "Good king, thank you."

"For doing what?" the puzzled king asked as he turned back in the doorway.

"Not for what you have done, but for what you have *not* done. Thank you for *not* throwing spears, for not rebelling against kings, for not exposing a man in authority when he was vulnerable, for not dividing a kingdom, for not attacking young Absaloms who look very much like young Davids but aren't."

He paused. "And thank you for suffering, for being willing to lose everything. Thank you for giving God a free hand to end and even destroy your Kingdom if it pleases Him. Thank you for being an cxamplc to us all.

"And most of all," he chuckled, "thanks for not consulting witches."

Chapter XXIV

"I thank you for coming, Zadok."

"My king."

"You are a priest of God: Could you tell me a story of long ago?"

"What story, my king?"

"Do you know the story of Moses?"

"I do."

"Tell it to me."

"It is long; shall I tell it all?"

"No, not all."

"Then what part?"

"Tell me about Korah's rebellion."

The high priest stared at David with eyes burning. David stared back, his also ablaze. The two men understood.

"I shall tell you the story of Korah's rebellion, and of Moses' behavior in the midst of that rebellion."

"Many men have heard the story of Moses. He is the supreme example of the Lord's anointed. God's true government rests upon a man, no, upon the contrite heart of a man. There is no form or order to God's government; there is only a man with a contrite heart. Moses was such a man.

"Korah was not such a man, although he was the first cousin of Moses. Korah wanted the authority Moses had. One peaceful morning, Korah awoke. There was no discord among God's people that morning, but before the day was over, he had found 252 men to agree with his charges against Moses."

"Then there were problems in the nation when Moses ruled?" asked David.

"There are always problems in kingdoms," replied Zadok. "Always. The ability to see faults is a common and a cheap gift."

David smiled and asked, "But Zadok, you know there have been unjust kingdoms and unjust rulers and pretenders and liars who have ruled and governed. How can a simple people tell which is a kingdom with faults, but led by men of God, and which is a kingdom unworthy of submission? How can a people know?"

David stopped; he realized that he had hit upon what he wished to know. Heavily, he spoke again. "And the king—how can he know? Are there signs?'' David's final words were anxious.

''You are looking for some list let down from heaven, David. Even if there were such a list, even if there were a way to know, wicked men would arrange their kingdoms to fit the list! And if there were a list and a good man filled it to perfection, there would be those declaring he had fulfilled not one qualification listed therein. You underestimate the human heart, David.''

''Then how shall the people know?''

''They shall not.''

''You mean that in the midst of a hundred voices making a thousand claims, the simple people of God have no assurance of who is truly anointed to bear God's authority and who is not?''

''They shall never be certain.''

''Who, then, can know?''

''God always knows—but He does not tell.''

''Then is there no hope for those who must follow unworthy men?''

''Their grandchildren will be able to see the matter clearly. They will know. But those caught up in the drama? They shall never be certain. Nonetheless, a good thing will come from it all.''

"What is that?''

''As surely as the sun rises, men's hearts will be tested. Despite the many claims—and counter claims—the hidden motives within the hearts of all involved will be revealed. This may not seem important in the eyes of men, but in the eyes of God and angels such things are central.

"I despise such tests,'' replied David wearily. "I hate such nights. Yet He seems to send many, many things into my life to test this heart of mine. Once more this night, I find my heart is on trial.

''Zadok, there is something that bothers me above all else. Perhaps God *is* finished with me. Is there not some way for me to know?''

'I know of no other ruler in all history who would even ask the question, good king. Most other men would have ripped their opponent— or even their imagined opponent—to shreds by now. But to answer your question, I know of no way for you to be certain that God is—or is not—finished with you.''

David sighed, and choked back a sob. "Then continue with the story. Korah had 252 followers, did he? What happened next?''

"Korah approached Moses and Aaron with his troop. He informed Moses that he had no right to all the authority he exercised."

"Well, we Hebrews are consistent, aren't we?" laughed David.

"No, the heart of man is consistent, David," replied Zadok.

"Tell me, what was Moses' response to Korah?"

"At 40, Moses had been an arrogant, self-willed man, not unlike Korah. At 80, he was a broken man. He was . . . ."

"The meekest man who ever lived," interrupted David.

"The man who carries the rod of God's authority should be. Yes, a broken man faced Korah. And I believe you already know what Moses did, David. He did . . . nothing."

"Nothing. Ah, what a man."

"He fell on his face before God. That is all he did."

"Why did he do that, Zadok?"

"David, you of all men must know. Moses knew God alone had put him in charge of

Israel. There was nothing that needed to be done. Those 253 men would seize the kingdom—or God would vindicate Moses. Moses knew that."

"Men find it hard to imitate such a life, do they not? Especially in such a hard moment. But tell me, how did God vindicate Moses?"

"Moses told the men to return the next day with censers and incense . . . and God would decide the issue."

"So!" cried David. "So!" he exclaimed again even louder. "Sometimes God *does* tell," he said excitedly. "What happened next?"

"Korah and two of his friends were swallowed by the earth. The other 250 died by . . . ."

"Never mind. Suffice it to say that Moses was proven to be in authority . . . by God! God *did* tell! The people knew who really had authority from God, and at last, Moses had rest."

"No, David. He did not find rest, and the people were not satisfied with God's answer! The very next day the whole congregation murmured against Moses and would all have died perhaps, except for the prayers of Moses."

"And men fight to become kings!" David shook his head in perplexity.

Zadok paused, then continued: "David, I

perceive you are torn by the question of what is true authority and what is not. You want to know what to do with a rebellion, if indeed it is a rebellion and not the hand of God. I trust you will find the only pure thing to do and do it. Thereby you will teach us all.''

The door opened. Abishai rushed in. ''Good king! Your son, you own flesh and blood, has proclaimed himself *king* in Hebron. At first impression, it seems all Israel has gone over to him. He plans to take the throne. He marches toward Jerusalem. Some of the men closest to you have gone over to him.''

David walked away. He spoke something to himself but beyond the ears of any other. ''Israel's third king? Do true leaders of the Kingdom of God come about thusly?''

Zadok, not certain if he should be hearing David's words or not, spoke out. ''My king?''

David turned. His eyes were moist.

''At last,'' said David quietly, ''at last this matter will be resolved. Perhaps tomorrow someone besides God will know.''

''Perhaps,'' said Zadok, ''but perhaps not. Such questions may be debated even after we are all dead.''

''That might still be tomorrow,'' laughed David. ''Go, Abishai, tell Joab. You will find him in the turret of the east wall.''

81

Abishai departed as he had entered, in haste
and in fury.

"I wonder, Zadok," mused David, "if a man
can force God into a position where He *must*
tell."

Chapter XXV

Abishai rushed across the courtyard into the
open door at the base of the east rampart and
charged up the spiral staircase. Inside, at the
top of the stair, Joab stared down at him. Then
he reached for a torch and began rushing
down. In the flickering light of the torches,
they met, each studying the face of the other
intently. Then Abishai spoke.

"Have you heard, Joab?"

"Heard! 'Tis midnight, yet half the city is
awake with the word. How can it be, Abishai—
a son against his own father!"

"When kingdoms are vulnerable, men see
queer sights," responded Abishai with a
distant stare.

"And will sacrifice anything to satisfy
ambition," added Joab angrily. "What think
you of these things, Abishai?"

"What think I?" responded Abishai, matching
Joab's anger with his own rage. "This!
Absalom has no authority in the kingdom. He
holds no power, no office, yet he has risen up
to divide the kingdom. He has raised his hand
against the very anointed of God—against
David! David—who has never done or spoken
one evil word against him.

"What think I?" Abishai's voice rose toward a crescendo. "This: If Absalom, who has no authority, will commit this deed; if Absalom, who is nothing, will divide the very kingdom of God;" his voice now rolled like thunder, "man, if Absalom will do these things *now*, what in the name of sanity might that man do if he be *king?*"

Chapter XXVI

David and Zadok were alone once more.

"And now, what shall you do, David? In your youth, you spoke no word against an unworthy king. What shall you do now with an equally unworthy youth?"

"As I said," replied David, "these are the times I hate the most, Zadok. Nonetheless, against all reason, I judge my own heart first and rule against its interests. I shall do what I did under Saul. I shall leave the destiny of the Kingdom in God's hands alone. It may be that He is finished with me. Perhaps I have sinned too greatly and am no longer worthy. Only God knows if that is true, and it seems He will not tell." Then, clenching his fist, yet with a touch of wry humor in his voice, he added emphatically, "But today I shall give circumstances ample space for this untelling God of ours to be found out. I know of no other way to bring that about except by doing nothing. The throne is not mine. Not to take, not to protect, and not to keep.

"I shall leave the city. The throne is the Lord's. So is the kingdom. I will do nothing. I will not hinder God. No obstacle, no activity on my part lies in the space between God and His will. He has no hindrance to prevent Him from His will. Now it is possible. God shall be God!"

The true king turned and walked quietly out of
the throne room, out of the palace, out of the
city. He walked and he walked . . . .

Into the bosoms of all men whose hearts
are pure.

Well, dear reader, the time has come for us to say goodbye once more. I will leave you to your thoughts and to reflection on the hidden motives of your own heart.

I trust, by the mercy of God, that we shall meet again.

Also by Gene Edwards

The Divine Romance

If you have enjoyed *A Tale of Three Kings,* you will wish to read Gene Edwards' powerful and compelling book, *The Divine Romance,* his best book to date. A story of un-imaginable sweep and beauty. The greatest love story ever told, unfolding the deepest and most profound truths of the Christian faith in the simplicity of storytelling.   12.95 cloth

Our Mission

Edwards faces the complex problem of splits in Chris-tian groups, and raises a new standard of conduct for those found in the midst of division.   9.95

Letters to A Devastated Christian

A companion volume to *A Tale of Three Kings,* a series of letters written to a Christian who is on the verge of bitterness because of his experience in an authoritarian movement. Edwards offers counsel, objective understand-ing of the events, a way of healing, and points the Christian once more to Christ.   3.95

A Tale of Three Kings is also available in French   4.95

A Tale of Three Kings

Gene Edwards is a native Texan. He graduated from East Texas State University at 18, with majors in history and literature. His seminary studies in Ruschlikon, Switzerland and at Southwestern Baptist in Fort Worth led to a Master's Degree in theology at age 22. He and his wife Helen presently make their home in Quebec, Canada.

The cover illustration, "Saul Attempts the Life of David" is by Gustave Dore, c.1866. The cover and text of this book were designed by B. Barrett. The text was typeset by Aslan Typesetting, Isla Vista, California, and the display type is by Roger Graphics, Santa Barbara, California.

The text type is 11 point English Roman and the display typeface is Zapf Bold Italic.

Christian Books puts out a catalogue each year. The following are the books and prices for 1984 only. Write for a free catalogue with updated prices.

Let us know if you would like to receive notification of future publications. (Christian Books also sponsors a conference on the deeper Christian life each summer.)

Books on the Deeper Christian Life

Practicing His Presence, *Brother Lawrence*	4.95
The Spiritual Guide, *Michael Molinos*	5.95
Divine Life, *Mary McDonough*	5.95
Fenelon's Spiritual Letters	5.95
Experiencing the Depths of Jesus Christ, *Guyon*	4.95
Guyon's Spiritual Letters	6.95
Spiritual Torrents, *Guyon*	9.95

Books on Church History

The Early Church, *Gene Edwards*	4.95
Torch of the Testimony, *John W. Kennedy*	6.95
(The story of the church in the dark ages)	

Devotional books (from Jeanne Guyon's devotional commentary on the Bible)

Genesis	5.95
Song of Songs	5.95

Also

Madame Guyon's Life, *Upham*	9.95

Order from your favorite Christian Bookstore

or

Christian Books
Box 959
Augusta, Maine 04330
207-582-4880